Cool Guide to

Puerto Escondido

Food • Wellness • Music

Join our travel community and sign up for our next adventures:

🌐   www.coolguidetravel.com

The Inside Scoop

FOOD 8

   Served á la Table 8
      Cafés & Brunch Options 9
      Co-Working Cafés w/ Speed 13
      Food Courts 18
      Restaurants 21
      Vegan & Vegetarian 25
   DIY at Home 28
      Organic Markets 29
      Organic Food Shops 31

DRINKS 34

   Cocktails & Beer 35
   Mezcales 38

PARTY 40

   Early Night 41
   Late Night 43

WELLNESS 46

   Movement 47
   Fitness 50
   Surf Classes 52

COOL
GUIDE TRAVEL

Massage	54
Spiritual	56
Hair & Make-Up	58
Tattoo	60
Beach Clubs	62

ART & DESIGN 64

Cool Clothing	65

CO-WORKING 68

Cool Co-Working Spaces	69

EXCURSIONS 72

DIY Tours - Close	73
DIY Tours - Far	76
Guided Tours	78

SLEEP 82

Fancy	83
Mexican	85

PUERTO ESCONDIDO

The 4 main areas of Puerto Escondido

Rinconada / Bacocho: Lovely neighborhood with colonial style houses, a boulevard with restaurants and cafés, a relaxed vibe, plus several beaches for swimming (Bacocho, Carrizalillo, Manzanillo).

Centro: The downtown of Puerto, with shops for all necessities, plus one big Chedraui supermarket (the Mexican Wallmart), lots of traditional Mexican restaurants at the Adoquin and the fisherman's beach Playa Principal.

Zicatela: Long stretched beach only for surfing, not for swimming, with lots of restaurants, beach bars, tourist shops and three beach night clubs.

La Punta: The surfer / fomo area of town with a long stretched beach and plenty of restaurants and cafés, hipster shops, two beach clubs, and everybody in their bikinis or yoga pants all day long.

Puerto Escondido

The best of food, wellness, music, art & design

Puerto Escondido has been known to surfers since a long time for its world-record-big waves, secluded beaches along the coast for sunbathing and a relaxed vibe that still feels like a village, yet offers more of a city.

Puerto is a big mixture. For one part, it's very touristy, since people from Mexico City come here for a weekend get-away with all night-long parties. At the same time, Puerto offers a zen-vibe, because of its secluded spots in nature, where you only get by dirt road. And then there is the sexy surfer crowd that hits the waves every morning and drives around with their surf board.

Puerto has it all: From fitness at the beach, to yoga at the rooftop, to wellness, good food, electronic parties and sunset vibes. It even has a few co-working spaces now, so that more and more digital nomads are flocking to this tiny beach town. Although the Wi-Fi is pretty spotty most of the time, it's getting better in certain areas, which again gives it its unique charm. How many places on earth are left where the Wi-Fi is bad and the vibes are so natural?

More and more shops are opening that bring in the style of Tulum, and even the restaurants' scene is multicultural, from Vietnamese, to Middle Eastern, Mexican, Vegan, Thai and Ayurveda, everything has its place here.

Plus, Puerto has some of the best excursions to offer! If you are coming to this surf town for the first time, you'll find that there is so much to discover! Whale watching, dolphin and turtle swimming, horse rides to the hot springs, bioluminescent waters at night, the freeing of baby turtles at sunset, and much more!

Come visit Puerto Escondido and find out what it's all about!

Cafés & Brunch Options

Rinconada / Bacocho

Dulce Tierra Bakery & Coffee Shop

- 📍 Boulevard Rinconada s/n, Rinconada
- 🕐 Mo – Sat 7 – 8pm, Sunday 8 – 4pm
- 🌐 @dulcetierrabakery

Sweet little café (in the literal sense) with lots of options for freshly baked and delicious pastries (also vegan), cakes and sweets, as well as sandwiches and the like, coffee and juices. They have another branch in La Punta, too, which is even more busy than this one! The terrace upstairs is worth to hang out for a while and just chill among a lot of plants.

La Isla *DJ

- 📍 Manzanillo Beach, Rinconada
- 🕐 Mo – Sun 12pm – 8pm
- 🌐 @laislabeachclub

One of the most underrated places to eat, relax and have a good cocktail. Delicious fruit bowls, poké bowls, fruits in chocolate sauce, juices and delightful cocktails. Awesome presentation and one of the most beautiful, serene spots at the beach. They have hammocks, pillows to chill on, beach chairs, and rather Ibiza kind of flair. DJs every day from 2pm – 8pm.

Zicatela

Spirulina

📍 Avenida las Brisas, Zicatela

⏱ Wed – Sat 8am – 10pm, Tuesday closed

🌐 @spirulina_juicebar

One of the best places for freshly made juices (that are so delicious!) with superfoods, delicious breakfast (including peanut butter wholewheat toast), bliss balls, Mexican food, vegan options and a good vibe. It gets busy during the day with surfers, digital nomads and yogis (there is a yoga shala above), but it's really just to enjoy the food and good company here, since the Wi-Fi doesn't work too well.

Elephant Garden & Kankedami Shop

📍 At the end of the passage de la Iguana, corner to Av. Del Morro, Zicatela

⏱ Mon – Sun 8am – 1:30pm

🌐 @elephantgardenpuertoescondido

The best morning brunch spot in town, which is so loved, that you need to come early or wait, until you get a table in the garden. They offer a wide variety of vegan and vegetarian dishes, coffee, juices, and lattes in a beautiful presentation. There is also an organic / art shop in the entrance to Elephant Garden.

Bagetteria Zicatela

- 📍 Avenida del Morro, Zicatela
- 🕒 Tue – Sun 9am – 6pm, Monday closed
- 🌐 @baguetteria.puerto

This little 3 table joint has the best sandwiches, baguettes (vegan options with tofu), salads, coffee and especially home-made vegan ice cream (with almond or coconut milk, red berries or tropical fruits) in town! It has a perfect view to the beach too, so great for a snack.

La Punta

Dulce Tierra

- 📍 Heroes Oaxaceños 33, La Punta
- 🕒 Mon – Sun 7:30am – 8pm
- 🌐 @dulcetierrabakery

This café gets so crowded, it's really a hotspot (even if the Wi-Fi hotspot is not so strong). They offer a range of delicious pastries, cakes and coffee, and are situated just around the corner of the main road that leads down to the beach.

Co-Working Cafés w/ Speed

Centro

Café Losodeli & Co-Working

📍 Prolongación de Calle Segunda Nte. s/n, Centro

🕐 Mon – Sun 7:30am – 2:30pm

🌐 @cafelosodeli

This café, run by a family from Puerto Escondido, is highly popular, for one, because it serves delicious healthy food, but also attached to it is a digital nomad hostel, that offers co-working spaces (you can also just pay for a day or a week), a pool and a relaxing garden. It's a very well-designed spot that harmonizes you instantly, once you arrive.

Café La Fé

📍 Av. Alfonso Pérez Gasga 106, Centro

🕐 Tue – Sat 8am – 6pm, Sunday / Monday closed

🌐 @micafelafe

This little café with 6 individual tables inside and a little yard with a few more tables is a conscious / religious space (fé means faith) offers delicious home-made vegan and non-vegan bakery, coffee, food and the fastest Wi-Fi in town. It gets busy, so come early! They also sell beautiful Macramé.

Rinconada / Bacocho

Café Choc

- 📍 Benito Juárez 15, Rinconada
- 🕐 Mon – Sat 7am – 9pm, Sundays closed
- 🌐 FB @cafechocpuertoescondido

This little gem is perfect for a good morning coffee, lots of home-made cake (not vegan, unfortunately!), or a fruit juice. The service is fast, the atmosphere relaxed and the Wi-Fi very fast for up- and downloads. You have several single tables that are perfect for work. Or, read a book from the extensive library inside (ordered by languages). Café Choc is just before the passage that leads down to Carizalillo Beach.

Zicatela

Amarisa & Selina   ** Live Music / DJ*

- 📍 Avenida del Morro 4, Zicatela
- 🕐 Mon – Sun 7am – 9pm
- 🌐 @amarisacafe I @selina

Beautiful small café attached to Selina Hostel and Co-Working, which has pretty stable Wi-Fi, pastries, as well as delicious sandwiches. If Selina gets too loud or too crowded, you can come here and work with relative tranquility (even though the few tables are taken fast). Other than that, Selina has a dedicated co-working space upstairs, which fills up quickly, according to season, but on the weekends and evenings it's always empty.

Olas Altas Restaurant

- 📍 Avenida del Morro / Las Olas, Zicatela
- 🕒 Wed – Mon 7am – 11pm, Tue 7:30am - 11pm
- 🌐 @hotel_surf_olasaltas

Small pizza restaurant on the main tourist street of Zicatela that belongs to a hotel, which has surprisingly good Wi-Fi, better than in other places. The food is not the best, but if you are in the area and need a place to work, try this one. It's not very well frequented, so you usually get a table.

La Punta

El Petit Café – French Bakery and Café

- 📍 Highway / Alejandro Cardenas Peralta, next to the 7+1, La Punta
- 🕒 Mon – Sat 7am – 6:30pm
- 🌐 @elpetitcafe_puerto

Small café with French pastries and coffee, with just a handful of tables and delicious food, that's perfect for co-working. Come early to get your spot. They have a small organic store attached.

N'duva Café

📍 Alejandro Cárdenas Peralta s/n, next to Punta Paradiso Cabanas, close to beach, La Punta

🕐 Mo – Sun 8am – 6:30pm

🌐 @nduvacafe

This small café sells organic coffee from Pluma de Hidalgo region, pastries and sandwiches, and you'll always be up-to-date with the latest wellness offerings from the posters on the outside walls of it. It does have better Wi-Fi than most places, and you can supposedly even have calls for work here. Due to their outdoor seating being open to the main tourist stretch, and just one table inside, it gets a little noisy at times, though.

Amarisa Café

📍 Heroes Oaxaqueños s/n / Nayarit, La Punta

🕐 Mo – Sun 7am – 9pm

🌐 @amarisacafe

Beautiful space with several tables on their terrace and inside, individual work space and longer tables for a group, with even comfy pillows and a bright spacious feel to it! You get everything from delicious home-made pastries, to smoothie bowls, sandwiches and more, and of course coffee, tea and juices. Great place to work, just the music can be distracting at times.

Food Courts

Zicatela

Mar & Wana *DJ*

📍 Av. del Morro, behind Piedra de la Iguana, Zicatela

🕒 Sun / Tue - Thur 5pm - 2am, Fri / Sat 5pm - 5am, Monday closed

🌐 @marandwana

A unique boho food court and cocktail bar that is set in a lush jungle setting, with hidden upstairs viewpoint on a wooden dock to see the sunset. Enjoy a meal on wooden tables and benches, surrounded by Tulum-style Macramé under the shade of huge trees. Mainly burgers, tacos and some vegan options here. Great for exclusive dinners with exclusive deco, an evening with friends or an early nighter that blends into a party, when the DJs start at midnight.

La Punta

El Arbol *Live Music*

📍 Alejandro Cárdenas Peralta s/n, after Tamaulipas, La Punta

🕒 Mon – Thu 7pm – 12am, Fri / Sat 6pm – 12am, Sunday closed

🌐 @elarbol.thetree

Open Air organic and cultural food court, with pizza, vegan burgers, tacos, Thai food, and more, with live music and DJs most days and sometimes even salsa classes! The vibe is great, and the food is the best.

Espacio Cometa *Live Music / DJ*

📍 Alejandro Cárdenas Peralta / Brisas, La Punta

🕐 Fri – Wed 6 – 11pm, Thursday closed

🌐 @espacio_cometa

Espacio Cometa is a beautiful garden and food court in a delightful nature spot, that offers juices, coffee, crêpes, pizza, omelettes, Thai and Mexican food, and of course cocktails and beers for later at night! They also bring DJ's and live music on certain evenings. It's a wrap.

Punta Origen *Live Music / DJ*

📍 Puebla 48 / Brisas, La Punta

🕐 Tue – Sun 3 – 11pm, Monday closed

🌐 @puntaorigen

Punta Origen is a lively food court, with lots of food options from empanadas, to burgers (vegan too), Mexican food, as well as Sushi. Of course, you'll also get the best cocktails in town here, a stellar ambience, and on Thursdays they host the booked out Open Mic Nights, with local musicians and anyone with a talent. All of Puerto Escondido comes here.

Rinconada / Bacocho

Almoraduz, Cocina de Autor

- 📍 Benito Juárez 12, Rinconada
- 🕒 Mon – Sun 1pm – 10pm | Upscale
- 🌐 @almoraduzpuerto

Very popular joint in Rinconada, which convinces with its specialty food, high-quality chef, and a classy setting. Even though the area is surf oriented, this little place got style, an impeccable presentation of the dishes, and highly trained staff! Not to be missed.

La Pasteleria il Pastaio

- 📍 Benito Juárez, Rinconada
- 🕒 Sat – Thu 3pm – 10pm, Fri 3pm – 11:30pm | Pizza

The absolute best handmade pizza and pasta in this corner of town, with real Italian feel and flavor to it! They do everything in-house, the pasta dough too! At very reasonable prices, with a delightful presentation of the dishes, so it's a no-brainer.

La Punta

Lychee

- 📍 Alejandro Cárdenas Peralta, after Heroes Oaxaqueños
- 🕐 Mo – Sun 5pm – 11pm I Asian
- 🌐 @lycheethaifood

An earthy big space with a huge open kitchen, where you see your food being made right in front of your eyes! One of the few Asian spots in town, that's truly an experience. It gets crowded, so reserve or come early.

Fish Shack La Punta

- 📍 Alejandro Cárdenas Peralta s/n, between Heroes Oaxaqueños and Benito Juarez
- 🕐 Mo – Sun 1pm – 10pm I Mexican
- 🌐 @fishshacklapunta

One of the best fish taco places in town, which is confirmed by the crowds swarming into this little side street every day. They also offer a few vegan and vegetarian options of roasted vegetables, which come in a unique presentation - one of a kind in Puerto!

Moxie

📍 Alejandro Cárdenas Peralta, next to Alaburger up the stairs

⏱ Mon – Sat 6pm – 11pm, Sunday closed I Mexican

🌐 @moxie.escondido

A unique, stylish place (even with A/C, which is rare), from where you can see the sunset, enjoy a solid setting and receive "concina de autor" from Maria Hashimoto, with farm to table Omakase, a mixture of Japanese and Mexican ingredients, that are being sourced from local farms, and that you don't get anywhere else. It's a truly creative spot with exquisite natural wines too. They tell you all about the different ingredients in each dish. It's not à la carte, but by a set 4/5-course menu, including Mezcal tasting. One of the most underrated and hidden spots in Puerto! It's an experience.

Don Ramon

📍 Alejandro Cárdenas Paralta, after Justo Salvador Maldonado

⏱ Sat - Thu 9am - 11pm, Friday closed I Argentinian

The only and best little Argentinian gem in La Punta with original empanadas, including vegan and vegetarian options, and original Fernet con Coca Cola, a bitter herbal drink sweetened with Coke. This spot has just two tables and a wooden table on both side-walls with bar chairs, but is totally worth the visit for a snack.

Vegan & Vegetarian

Rinconada

El Sultan

- 📍 Benito Juárez / Pargo, Rinconada
- 🕐 Mon – Sat 8am – 10pm, Sunday closed | Middle Eastern
- 🌐 @sultan_puertoescondido

Hands down the most reasonably priced Middle Eastern restaurant in Puerto Escondido. Delicious hummus, falafel and a selection of Mexican dishes, drinks and more. It's not entirely vegan, but has several vegan options! They have a communal seating area, but also offer take-away.

Zicatela

Sativa *DJ*

- 📍 Avenida del Morro 5, Zicatela
- 🕐 Mo – Sun 10am – 10pm | Cosmopolitan
- 🌐 @sativapuerto

Relaxed atmosphere on the beach, great sunset views and delicious world cuisine in a bamboo setting! Be it vegan and vegetarian options like falafel, curry, salad, or one of their Mexican dishes, like shrimp tacos or ceviche, the presentation and taste are impeccable. They also have regular sunset DJ sessions and a volleyball court at the beach.

La Punta

Xocoyo

📍 Alejandro Cárdenas Peralta / Beach, La Punta

🕐 Tue – Sun 9am – 10pm, Monday closed I Vegan

🌐 @xocoyo.puertoescondido

An all veggie Mexican place that offers everything from Beyond Meat burgers, to tacos *al pastor* with seitan, quesadillas, burritos and more, all vegan and vegetarian! They also offer healthy juices and golden milk in their breakfast menu.

Persia

📍 Av. Alejandro Cárdenas 616, La Punta

🕐 Mon - Fri 7:30pm - 11:30pm I Middle Eastern

🌐 @persia_pxm

Another Middle Eastern restaurant with the most delicious falafel, hummus, taboulé and whatever your heart desires. The kicker is the original decoration, as if you were sitting in a desert tent. The place is extremely cosy, almost romantic, and the music fits the ambience, with oriental-electronics playing in the background. All food is prepared by the owners, a must visit in La Punta!

Organic Markets

Zicatela

Mercado Zicatela

📍 Carretera Costera, Santa Maria

🕐 Mon – Sun 7am – 7pm

Organic market with local produce, bakeries, juice shops, flowers, as well as artisanal shops and second-hand clothing, all at the best prices. It's an experience! You find everything you need to cook, decorate your home and dress yourself here.

La Punta

Frutas y Verduras de la Costa

📍 Alejandro Cárdenas Perralta / Brisas, La Punta

🕐 Mon – Sun 7am – 11pm

This fruit and vegetable shop has everything you might be looking for, including vegan deserts in the fridge. They also have spices, herbs and seeds. The outside wall gives you an overview of all upcoming wellness workshops.

Organic Food Shops

Rinconada / Bacocho

Puerto Verde Rinconada

📍 Benito Juárez 603A, Rinconada

🕐 Mon – Sat 8am – 8pm, Sunday closed

🌐 @verdepuerto

Small organic shop that offers superfood powders, natural cosmetics, organic fruits and vegetables, kombucha, fresh coconut water in bottles, pastries, plant based milks, and more. Great little local shop.

Canela

📍 Benito Juárez, between Marlín & Barracudas

🕐 Mo – Sun 9am - 7pm

🌐 @canelamercadonatural

This shop is amazing, as it has almost everything you can think of as refill options: seeds, grains, cacao, herbs, spices, granola, chai tea, you name it. They also have a section with natural cosmetics, air sprays, incense, palo santo, and vegan food. And extremely reasonably priced. So good! Their second branch is in Mercado Zicatela.

La Punta

Puerto Verde La Punta

- 📍 Alejandro Cárdenas Peralta, close to the Highway
- 🕐 Mon – Sat 8am – 8pm, Sunday closed
- 🌐 @verdepuerto

The counterpart to the small Rinconada shop has more superfoods and powders on offer, plus a lot of vegetables and fruits, fresh from their farm. Whatever you need, from nuts and seeds, to cacao, or cosmetics, it's all here.

Moringa Fresh & Wild

- 📍 End of Alejandro Cárdenas Peralta / at the beach
- 🕐 Mon – Sun 8am – 9pm

Great organic shop with everything from vegan desserts, to tofu and falafel, to superfoods, ceramic mate cups, smudging herbs, palo santo, essential oils, cosmetics, take-away and whatever else your hippie heart desires!

DRINKS

Cocktails & Beer

Rinconada

Puerto Brewing Company   *Live Music*

📍 Benito Juárez 306 / Puerto Manzanillo, Rinconada

🕐 Mon – Sat 4pm – 12am, Sunday closed

🌐 @puertobrew

One of the best breweries in town with a wide variety of home-made beer in different flavours (from the tap), as well as home-made kombucha, pineapple ferment, and cold brew coffee. Not to be missed. They also serve vegan cakes and vegan pizza now, and offer yoga and fitness classes in the morning, plus salsa lessons and live music in the evenings. The space alternatively serves as a co-working in the mornings when you get a daily / weekly or monthly pass.

Zicatela

La Palapita Bar

📍 Avenida del Morro, next to Xcaanda, Zicatela

🕐 Mon – Sun 11am – 12am

🌐 @palapitabar

The best spot right on a beach, with a cocktail bar looking like a pineapple, cozy low benches and sofas for a relaxed sunset evening, and the only vegan hot dog in town for only 45 Pesos (after 6pm). They serve delicious cocktails in Tiki mugs and the Piña Colada in the pineapple itself with a little umbrella on top, for very reasonable prices and a refill option of only 25 pesos.

La Punta

La Olita La Punta *DJ

📍 Alejandro Cárdenas Peralta, between Heroes Oaxaquennos & Benito Juárez, towards the beach

🕒 Fri - Wed 5pm – 12am

🌐 @laolitalapunta

Great concept bar on the beach, with a relaxed and organic atmosphere, with wooden tables and low benches, extraordinary cocktails, and very good tacos! They also have DJ sessions with a great selection of downtempo music.

Savanna Café & Mezcal *DJ

📍 Alejandro Cárdenas Peralta, at the beach, La Punta

🕒 Mon - Sun 9am – 12am

🌐 @savanna_mx

A huge space with upscale interior patio and a terrace upstairs, for drinks, the best sunset view of La Punta, and DJ session at 5pm every day! If you are lucky, you'll find a very well-known DJ come here to play an undercover set. They also offer a wide variety of food for breakfast, lunch and dinner from oatmeal pancakes to fish & chips.

Mezcales

La Punta

Juana Mezcala   *Live Music / DJ*

📍 Alejandro Cárdenas Peralta 940, La Punta

🕐 Tue – Sun 6pm – 12am

🌐 @juanamezcala

Big Mezcal and cocktail bar that also offers delicious Mexican and cosmopolitan dishes and DJ sets / live music at the weekends. The presentation is amazing, the vibe is high, and it gets easily crowded, so come early – or late, whatever fits best!

Zicatela

Cayuco Cocina & Mezcal

📍 Av. del Morro 4, before Selina, Zicatela

🕐 Tue – Sun 2pm – 10pm, Monday closed

🌐 @cayucoescondido

A beautiful spot right at the beach of Zicatela with the perfect view for sunset, the best fish and seafood dishes including an impeccable presentation, as well great cocktails and local Mezcal. Not to be missed for either drinks or food! It's top notch style and class such as in London or Paris, but for the fraction of the price.

PARTY

Early Night

Zicatela

Selina   *Live Music / DJ

- 📍 Avenida de Morro 5, Zicatela
- 🕐 Wed – Sun 9-10pm
- 🌐 @selina

Live Music in the restaurant in the evenings at around 9 / 10pm, ranging from reggae to funk and DJ session with electronic music upstairs in the bar, later in the evening from 10pm. Check their announcements in the WhatsApp group (which you get at reception) or check their announcement board!

La Punta

El Bicho   *Live Music / DJ

- 📍 Querétaro / Beach, La Punta
- 🕐 Tue – Sun 9am – 11pm, Monday closed
- 🌐 @elbicho.lapunta

One of the best restaurants at the beach to watch the sunset, listen to either live or DJ music, and have a good beer, cocktail or decent sized portion of fish. Perfect for a romantic meet-up, or a beachy dinner with friends.

Late Night

Zictatela

Cactus Beach Club *DJ

- 📍 Avenida del Morro, Zicatela
- 🕐 Fri / Sat / Mon 10pm – 5am
- 🌐 @cactusbeachclub @bluemonday @cencalli

This infamous club has house music all night long from Thursday to Monday. Most well-known for their Blue Monday nights, where all of Puerto meets with local legends Heck and dbasser. They often invite foreign or well-known Mexican DJs to their club nights, so it gets good. Open Air and Berlin feel to it, with fire shows etc. Come before midnight and get in for free.

La Piedra de la Iguana *DJ

- 📍 Avenida del Morro, Zicatela
- 🕐 Fri / Sat – 11pm - sunrise
- 🌐 @piedradelaiguana

The after-hour place. Also, a beach club just opposite from Cactus, the vibe is different, more of a darkish, drug-laden spot when everything else closes. The sound is geared towards techno and freaky house, if that's a genre, but it has its own fire pit and a viewpoint on some rocks, plus they invite national and international talent to the stage. But here, come late, like really late, because early it's just an empty space with an open bar.

La Punta

Punta Vida *DJ

- 📍 Callejón Coahuila / Beach, La Punta
- 🕐 Fri / Sat 8pm – 12pm, Sun 5pm - 11pm
- 🌐 @_puntavida

Sundays are for BBQs at Punta Vida. Then this small space at the beach in an unfinished building gets packed with all of Puerto, and with local legend DJ's electronic tunes. Entry is free and the mood is good. Fridays and Saturdays has parties too, but rather irregular and not every party is busy, so it depends on the organizers.

Hucanii *DJ

- 📍 Chiapas / Beach, La Punta
- 🕐 Mon - Fri 5pm - 12am, Sat 7pm - 6am, Sundays closed
- 🌐 @hucanii.puertoescondido

This little restaurant / pizza / sushi place with cocktails and roof terrace turns into a club on Saturdays, and has either local talent or sometimes international DJs come to play. The sound system is not very good, and the vibe gets quite dark, but depending on the night the music can be groovy. They offer cinema with free popcorn on Mondays, special food nights during the week, as well as other occasional events, like an African beach party.

Wellness

Movement

Zicatela

Marea Yoga Studio

📍 Eucaliptos, Los Tamarindos, Zicatela

🕐 Mon - Fri 8am, Mon – Sun 9:30am, 11:30am, 6pm

🌐 @mareayogastudio

Beautiful natural open air yoga studio surrounded by palm trees, that offers a wide variety of classes from Aerial, to Vinyasa, Hatha, Kundalini, Yin, Acro Yoga and the occasional handstand workshop, cacao ceremony, or new moon circle.

Jardin Ganesha

📍 Fresnos, between Nogales & Zicatela Beach

🕐 Mon – Sat 9am / 6:30pm, Sun 10am

🌐 @jardinganesha

This beautiful hidden spot in Zicatela was founded by Beto Nijananda, a world traveler and devoted yoga teacher, who created a peaceful yoga garden with wooden cabins to stay for vacation, a light-filled and beautifully decorated yoga space and traditional yoga classes.

La Punta

Yoga One Love

📍 Tamaulipas between Baja California Norte & Baja California Sur

🕐 Mo – Fr 7:30am, Mo – Sun 9:30am, Sat / Sun 11:30

🌐 @yogaonelovepe

Awesome rooftop studio close to the beach with lots of space and many classes, mainly Vinyasa and Power Yoga though. It's one of the few studios that's starting already at 7:30am. Yoga One Love is attached to One Love Hostel and therefore is always well frequented. The weekend has workshops and Acro Yoga.

Casa de Olas

📍 Michoacan, La Punta

🕐 Tue, Thu, Fri 8:30am, Mon – Sun 10am, 11:30am, Fri 4pm, Mon – Thu 5pm, Fri 5:30pm, Mon – Wed 6:30pm

🌐 @casadeolas

Boutique Hotel with a pool and relaxed garden space, and the Element Fitness Shala on the rooftop. They offer more than just yoga, but also HIIT workouts, boxing, and surfers stretch classes, plus the infamous SHRED workouts, known all over Puerto.

Fitness

Zicatela

Paradise Gym

- 📍 Av. del Morro, opposite from Seline, Zicatela
- 🕒 Mon – Fri 7:15am, 8:30am, 9:30am, 5:30pm, Mon – Wed 8am, Fri 8:15am, Tu / Thu 4:30pm / 6pm, Wed / Thu 5:30pm
- 🌐 @paradisegym

Unique eco fitness centre right at the beach, leveraging the challenge of work-outs in the sand. All constructions and materials are made of wood, or did you ever try weight lifts with Fred Firestone weights? They do have an upstairs floor as well, for yoga and other classes. HIIT, Acro Yoga, SHRED, pole dance, body balance, boxing, it's all here. And – the gym is pet friendly, so bring your little friend!

Rinconada

CrossFit 954

- 📍 Morelos / Puerto Angelito, Rinconada
- 🕒 Mon, Wed, Fri 6am – 1pm, 5pm – 9pm
  Tue, Thu 6am – 11am, 5pm – 9pm
  Sat 9am – 11am, Sunday closed
- 🌐 @crossfit954

Amazing little gym with great equipment, cheerful and friendly coaches, and a "you can do it" attitude! Any age is welcome to start at Crossfit here, and lots of people not only leave with more muscle strength and higher fitness goals, but also with a bunch of new friends.

Surf Classes

Rincondada

Oasis Surf & Spanish School

📍 Benito Juarez 6, Rinconada

🕐 Mon – Sat 8am – 5pm, Sunday closed

📞 +52 – 954 582 1445

The best place to start your surf journey in Puerto, when you also want to make some friends and just get all inclusive: professional surf lessons, accomodation, yoga, surf photos and a grat team taking care of you. A lot of people come back, since they love the vibe so much. The team goes the extra mile to drive to distant less crowded beaches, too, if high season leaves no room for newbies in the water. You can book single lessons too.

La Punta

Chingon Surf Lessons

📍 C/ Puebla, between Brisas and Justo Salvador Maldonado, La Punta

🕐 Mon – Fri 7am – 1pm, Saturday & Sunday closed

📞 +52 – 954 161 2246

One of the best surf schools in the lively La Punta area, the main surf spot for beginner to intermediate, where the beach is long, and the waves can be strong. However, a lot of beginners start here, since the rocks at the end of the beach, soften the waves. You get 1:1 attention from the professional and lovely team around Javier & Pablo, who make sure that you already catch waves on the first day.

Massage

Rinconada / Bacocho

Japanese Massage

📍 Boulevard Benito Juárez, Rinconada

📞 +52 - 9541011319

One of the best massages in this corner of the beach. You can book a deep tissue or a highly recommended Shiatsu massage for 700 pesos 1h or 1000 for 1.5h. They are often booked, so ask for an appointment via WhatsApp or in person before you go.

Zicatela

Massage Fabi Arroche, Rockaway Hotel

📍 Av. del Morro, Zicatela

⏱ +52 – 9541566878

Great therapist from Mexico with deep tissue and Shiatsu massage, a beautiful space and added CBD, if you wish. She is often booked out in advance, so reserve via Whatsapp.

Spiritual

Zicatela

Temazcalli

- 📍 Temascalli / Infraganti, Lazaro Cardenas, Zicatela
- 🌐 https://temazcalli.com I contactotemazcalli@gmail.com
- 🌐 @temazcalli

Beautiful space away from the hustle and bustle that offers traditional sweat lodge ceremonies (Temazcal), as well as beauty treatments and massages.

Crystal World

- 📍 Av. del Morro, close to Selina, Zicatela
- 🕐 Mon – Sat 10am – 10pm, Sunday closed

Crystals from all over the world find their way here in all shapes and forms. Pointy quartz, raw quartz, heart-shaped crystals and many more. Nothing else, but this.

Hair & Make-Up

La Punta

Estética La Punta

📍 Alejandro Cárdenas Peralta, close to highway, La Punta

🕐 Mon – Sat 9am – 7pm, Sunday closed

Sweet little hair salon with only two chairs and two ladies working there, but they get the job done, and it's super cheap.

Rinconada

Karla Figueroa Salón & Spa

📍 2nda, De Cortes, close to Highway, between Cam. Carizalillo and Puerto Angelito, Rinconada

🕐 Mon – Sat 11am – 8pm, Sunday closed

Beauty salon and Spa that's highly frequented, because Karla is not only warm and welcoming, but also does an amazing job at her haircuts, hair dying, manicure and pedicure. It's and all around treatment.

Tattoo

La Punta

Irie Tattoo Shop

📍 Alejandro Cárdenas Peralta at the end, next to N'duva

⏱ Tue – Sun 12pm – 7pm, Monday closed

Great Tattoo Shop at the far en of the La Punta stretch, close to the surfers beach, and right next to N'duva Café. You can get everything from delicate fine lines to personalised designs here, done by the warm, zen and highly acclaimed artist Marysia.

Zicatela

Said Sutra Tattoo Artist

📍 Mercado Zicatela, Highway, Zicatela

⏱ Mon – Thu, Sat 9am – 7pm, Fri 9am – 9pm, Sunday closed

Very professional artist, specialized in fine line tattoo, delicate flowal designs, shades, and naturalistic images, up to abstract dotted images, fine lettering, and highly accurat.

Beach Clubs

Bacocho

Club de Playa Villasol

- 📍 Camino a Playa Bacocho
- 🕐 Mon – Sun 8am – 6pm
- 💰 800 pesos

Amazing beach club with a beautiful swimming pool, gardens, a restaurant and a bar. Very well selected African music, Afro House or smooth Latin sounds in the background, a volleyball court right on the beach and a tennis court for classes. If you want to avoid crowded beaches, or just need a smooth experience with a pool and showers, this is the spot. The entry price includes food and drink from the menu. Wednesdays they offer free cinema on a big screen on the beach!

Art & Design

Cool Clothing

Rinconada / Bacocho

Volt Surfwear

📍 Benito Juárez, local 14, Rinconada

🕐 Mon – Sun 10am – 8pm

🌐 @voltsurfwear

The first seamless surf wear for women of all ages, that can be adapted to any style you like, since the design is made to be reshaped and changed according to body type and design preference. They also have a few select dresses, Hawaii shirts, sexy tops and skirts.

Poema

📍 Benito Juárez, Rinconada

🕐 Mon – Sun 9am – 9pm

Designer linen skirts and tops from a Brazilian local designer, who honors the feminine and flowing soft materials. Earthen tones, simple cuts and belly free tops in a beautiful shop covered in green plants.

Zicatela

Camila's Boutique

📍 Bajada Brisas Zicatela, next to Garquiteg, Zicatela

🕐 Mon – Sun 10am – 8pm

Great little sports wear and surf wear shop with all the fancy brands, such as Roxy and O'Neill, with nice dresses, shorts, bikinis and not your usually cheap beach outfit from the tourist stalls. Truly selected items here.

R.M. Beach Boutique

📍 Av. del Morro, Zicatela

🕐 Mon – Sun 10am – 7pm

Great shop for unique bikini designs in floral prints, diverse colors and more, plus a few sexy sports bras that are made of very soft material and sit very well. It's more or less half-way into Av. del Morro after the first stretch of tourist shops.

La Punta

Sanddollar Label

📍 Héroes Oaxaqueños / Nuevo León, La Punta

🕐 Mon – Sun 10am – 8m

Tulum style shop and design label from Puerto Escondido, with hand-made feminine clothing, such as long flowy dresses, leopard skirts, animal print tops, sandals, bikinis and a few bags.

Raro Shop

📍 Alejandro Cárdenas Peralta, La Punta

🕐 Mon – Sun 10am – 10pm

Cool little shop with clothes from local designers that fit the beach, and hand-made journals for all occasions.

Co-Working

Cool Co-Working Spaces

Rinconada / Bacocho

Pauline Creative Hub

📍 Blvd Benito Juárez / Talxiaco, Bacocho

🕒 Mon – Fri 8am – 8pm, Sat 9am - 1pm

🌐 @paulinepxm

A recent addition to the co-working spaces in Puerto in a quieter area of town, this creative hub is located in a uniquely cool building that looks like a run down Moroccan Riad full of graffiti. It was a bowling spot before and in between functioned as a dark'n'dirty techno club. As a co-working it has a huge open space to work, plus a roof terrace, fast Wi-Fi and the hottest, mature co-workers, plus a lot of plants inside. More expensive than any other co-working with 300 pesos / day, 850 a week or 2500 a month, but the location is the deal.

Cowork Ñuu Rinconada

📍 Benito Juárez 47, Rinconada

🕒 Mo - Fri 9am - 6pm, Sat / Sun closed

📞 +52 954 100 8452

This very new co-working space looks almost like an Ikea apartment sporting a big sofa with pillows and TV, a balcony with chairs and plants, a huge kitchen, and long wooden desks, plus 3 private meeting rooms with A/C. Only monthly members are accepted at the moment, so send them a message to book a viewing. Once accepted, you get the keys though, and have access 24/7.

Zicatela

La Oficina del Puerto

- 📍 Av. del Morro / close to Bajada de Brisas, Zicatela
- 🕐 Mon – Sat 8am – 8pm, Sunday closed
- 🌐 @oficinadelpuerto

La Oficina del Puerto is a cute office on the first floor of a building on Avenida del Morro, close to Bajada de Brisas, with ocean view, several single desks, 2 video call cabins, a meeting room and endless coffee supply. 290 pesos / day and 1350 pesos / week, different monthly rates.

Selina

- 📍 Av. del de Morro, Zicatela
- 🕐 24/7
- 🌐 @selina

Selina is a hostel brand, so expect a very young crowd here, and it does get crowded. But they have a co-working upstairs that has a small booth for video calls and a bigger room with glass walls to the co-working space for meetings and video calls. Both of them are not entirely soundproof, so be aware of that. The co-working gets packed, since it comes included with the hostel packages from Selina, but it has fast Wi-Fi, and on the weekends and evenings it's practically empty. 200 pesos / day for the fast Wi-Fi pass at reception, different rates for work'n'stay.

Excursions

DIY Tours - Close

Zipolite

📍 Zipolite, Costa Oaxaqueña

🚌🚗 Collectivo van to San Antonio (direction Pochutla) (50 pesos), taxi from there to Zipolite (~ 200 pesos), or another collectivo (20 pesos)

Zipolite is best known for its nude beach and the big gay community. It has some really nice restaurants, cafés and good portion of nightlife, plus the parties are supposed to be better than in Puerto Escondido, more lively, colorful and fun! It's just shortly after Mazunte, so approximately 1.5 hours away. You can choose a simple accommodation or go for one of the upscale hotels on the beach, which invite to have a cozy romantic weekend get-away.

Mazunte

📍 Mazunte, Costa Oaxaqueña

🚌🚗 Collectivo van to San Antonion (direction Pochutla) (50 pesos), taxi from there to Mazunte (~ 200 pesos), or another collectivo (20 pesos)

Mazunte is a close-by town approximately an hour away from Puerto Escondido, that can easily be reached by collectivo van. People love Mazunte for its laid-back hippie vibe, the vast array of yoga, breathwork, and healing workshops, and the beautiful beaches with little waves, good to go for a swim. It's similar to Arambol Goa, live music at the beach in the afternoon, some bands playing in restaurants at night, and early wake-up in the morning for the yoga class.

Parque Nacional Lagunas de Chacahua

📍 Chacahua, Costa Oaxaqueña

🚌
🚗 Collectivo taxi to St. Rosa de Lima (90 – 160 pesos), shared taxi to Chacahua lagoon (50 pesos), boat trip to the beach (50 pesos), short trip by collectivo to town (20 pesos)

Chacahua is a laid back nature place at the Northern side of Puerto Escondido, that is loved by hippies and people looking for a peaceful get-away in a small village like location. You have to cross the lagoon by boat before you get to the actual beach. It's very small, just has a couple of huts on the beach, a few restaurants and a handful of shops. There is not much to do here, apart from taking a surf lesson, if the waves are higher, eating seafood, relaxing, or drinking Mezcal at night.

DIY Tours - Far

Oaxaca City – Street Art, Food, Cocktails

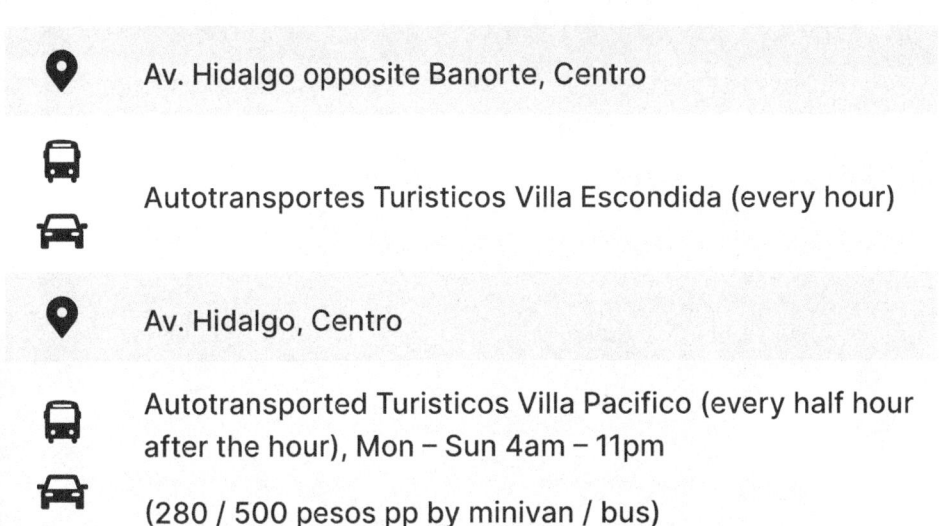

📍 Av. Hidalgo opposite Banorte, Centro

🚌🚗 Autotransportes Turisticos Villa Escondida (every hour)

📍 Av. Hidalgo, Centro

🚌🚗 Autotransported Turisticos Villa Pacifico (every half hour after the hour), Mon – Sun 4am – 11pm

(280 / 500 pesos pp by minivan / bus)

One of the most traditional cities in Mexico, with unique murals, authentic local food in all forms and fancy, plus outstanding cocktail creations and Mezcal bars. You also find lots of local art, pottery, clothes, Mexican fashion etc. here. Worth a weekend or a week-long trip. It's 8 hours by bus / van and 1 hour by flight.

Check out our Cool Guide to Oaxaca City, available on Amazon.

Guided Tours

These are the tours not to be missed while in Puerto Escondido. Most of them are being offered by Airbnb Experiences and by several tour operators in the center of Zicatela, where you can compare prices.

Whale & Dolphin Watching + Turtles

The whale mating season is in February / March, when you can easily spot one of these big mammals, sometimes even close to the beach. The tours also sport lots of dolphins in the hundreds, swimming next to your boat, and some sweet sea turtles floating along.

Bioluminescence at Night

This one is a special one at night. You meet your tour guide at 6 pm when he drives you and the other participants to the Manialtepec Lagoon. From there you take a short boat trip out into the open waters, to take a dip into the lagoon, which begins to sparkle like stardust, the moment you move your body. It's a thing.

Baby Turtle Release

This day-time activity is led by an NGO that helps to preserve the turtles on the beach, which come back every year to hatch their eggs here. Once the baby turtles left their shells, which are being protected by the NGO, tourist can come and take a baby turtle in a half coconut shell to release it on the beach, so it can find its way back into the ocean for its first open water swimming!

Horse Riding to Hot Springs

One of the more expensive trips, but so worth it. You are being brought to a place close to the lagoon of Manialtepec, from where you can mount the horses, after you've gotten a traditional taco made from the granny on the fire. From there you take a trip through grasslands, rivers and hidden path for approximately an hour, to finally reach natural sulfur hot springs somewhere inland. It's an experience. After one or two hours of lounging in the water, you trot back on the horseback, eat some more and then return with your driver to Puerto.

Skydiving over Puerto

A relatively recent addition to Puerto's fitness and wellness vibe as a guided "tour" is the option to go Skydiving over all of Puerto! You leave from the ground zone next to Casa de las Iguanas in Bajada de Brisas and join a group to take flight over Zicatela beach. Most people that've done it, come back with a big smile on their face and say it changed their life. Some people go on to become a skydiving trainer even. You can jump in tandem with a friend or an instructor, and will get a picture with your face in the wind. Contact Gio: +52-5528914700 for best prices.

SLEEP

Fancy

Casona Sforza

📍	La Barra, Santa Maria Colotepec
📞	+52 954 1685652
🌐	www.casonasforza.com I @casonasforza

One of the most impressive architectural pieces in the area, with unique rounded ceilings, eco-friendly design, and of course a pool. It's upscale (450 € / night), but being a peaceful haven outside of Puerto has its price. You can also come for the experience and enjoy their dinner creations in the restaurant.

Casa de Olas Boutique Hotel

📍	Michoacan, La Punta
📞	+52 954 688 4813 (Main) / +52 954 125 9342 (WhatsApp)
🌐	www.casadeolashotel.com I @casadeolaspuerto

Beautiful, and peaceful garden resort with a couple of rooms, a pool and delightful design. They offer health and fitness classes on the rooftop shala, delicious healthy food at their health bar, plus they have a tennis court next door.

Mexican

Villa Casalet

📍 Jacarandas / Jazmines Col., Zicatela

📞 +52 – 55 3627 7025

🌐 www.villacasalet.com.mx | @villacasaletpuertoescondido

Simple, bright and stylish Mexican hotel and villa with several rooms, some with ocean view, a whole villa to be rented and some apartments. It's close to the main strip in Zicatela, yet a bit hidden from it.

Villas Carrizalillo Hotel

📍 Cam. Carrizalillo, Rinconada

📞 +52 – 954 582 1735

🌐 www.villascarrizalillo.com | @villascarrizalillo

Big complex of several villas and apartments, most of them with their own pool, overlooking the beautiful Manzanillo beach. Quiet and peaceful with a gorgeous restaurant on site called "Espadin".

COOL
GUIDE TRAVEL

First Edition, 2022 © All rights reserved

The reproduction of the content of this Cool Guide to Puerto Econdido is strictly prohibited.

Cool Guide Travel is part of Cool Content Biz Ltd.

Printed in Great Britain
by Amazon